Juvenile Crime

Other Books in the Social Issues Firsthand Series:

SOCIAL ISSUES
FIRSTHAND

Juvenile Crime

Jill Hamilton, Book Editor

GREENHAVEN PRESS
A part of Gale, Cengage Learning

GALE
CENGAGE Learning™

Detroit • New York • San Francisco • New Haven, Conn • Waterville, Maine • London

GALE
CENGAGE Learning

Christine Nasso, *Publisher*
Elizabeth Des Chenes, *Managing Editor*

© 2009 Greenhaven Press, a part of Gale, Cengage Learning.

Gale and Greenhaven Press are registered trademarks used herein under license.

For more information, contact:
Greenhaven Press
27500 Drake Rd.
Farmington Hills, MI 48331-3535
Or you can visit our Internet site at gale.cengage.com

For product information and technology assistance, contact us at

Gale Customer Support, 1-800-877-4253
For permission to use material from this text or product, submit all requests online at www.cengage.com/permissions

Further permissions questions can be emailed to permissionrequest@cengage.com

Articles in Greenhaven Press anthologies are often edited for length to meet page requirements. In addition, original titles of these works are changed to clearly present the main thesis and to explicitly indicate the author's opinion. Every effort is made to ensure that Greenhaven Press accurately reflects the original intent of the authors. Every effort has been made to trace the owners of copyrighted material.

Cover photograph reproduced by image copyright Victoria Alexandrova, 2009. Used under license from Shutterstock.com.

LIBRARY OF CONGRESS CATALOGING-IN-PUBLICATION DATA

Juvenile crime / Jill Hamilton, book editor.
   p. cm. -- (Social issues firsthand)
   Includes bibliographical references and index.
   ISBN 978-0-7377-4387-6 (hardcover)
   1. Juvenile delinquency--United States. 2. Juvenile delinquents--United States.
   3. Juvenile corrections--United States. I. Hamilton, Jill.
   HV9104.J8317 2009
   364.360973--dc22
                                                        2008045608

Printed in the United States of America
2 3 4 5 6 7 13 12 11 10 09

Contents

Chapter 1: Reasons for Turning to Crime

Chapter 2: Punishments and Other Consequences

Chapter 3: Others Affected by Juvenile Crime

Foreword

Social issues are often viewed in abstract terms. Pressing challenges such as poverty, homelessness, and addiction are viewed as problems to be defined and solved. Politicians, social scientists, and other experts engage in debates about the extent of the problems, their causes, and how best to remedy them. Often overlooked in these discussions is the human dimension of the issue. Behind every policy debate over poverty, homelessness, and substance abuse, for example, are real people struggling to make ends meet, to survive life on the streets, and to overcome addiction to drugs and alcohol. Their stories are ubiquitous and compelling. They are the stories of everyday people—perhaps your own family members or friends—and yet they rarely influence the debates taking place in state capitols, the national Congress, or the courts.

The disparity between the public debate and private experience of social issues is well illustrated by looking at the topic of poverty. Each year the U.S. Census Bureau establishes a poverty threshold. A household with an income below the threshold is defined as poor, while a household with an income above the threshold is considered able to live on a basic subsistence level. For example, in 2003 a family of two was considered poor if its income was less than $12,015; a family of four was defined as poor if its income was less than $18,810. Based on this system, the bureau estimates that 35.9 million Americans (12.5 percent of the population) lived below the poverty line in 2003, including 12.9 million children below the age of eighteen.

Commentators disagree about what these statistics mean. Social activists insist that the huge number of officially poor Americans translates into human suffering. Even many families that have incomes above the threshold, they maintain, are likely to be struggling to get by. Other commentators insist that the statistics exaggerate the problem of poverty in the United States. Compared to people in developing countries, they point out, most so-called poor families have a high quality of life. As stated by journalist Fidelis Iyebote, "Cars are owned by 70 percent of 'poor' households. . . . Color televisions belong to 97 percent of the 'poor' [and] videocassette recorders belong to nearly 75 percent. . . . Sixty-four percent have microwave ovens, half own a stereo system, and over a quarter possess an automatic dishwasher."

However, this debate over the poverty threshold and what it means is likely irrelevant to a person living in poverty. Simply put, poor people do not need the government to tell them whether they are poor. They can see it in the stack of bills they cannot pay. They are aware of it when they are forced to choose between paying rent or buying food for their children. They become painfully conscious of it when they lose their homes and are forced to live in their cars or on the streets. Indeed, the written stories of poor people define the meaning of poverty more vividly than a government bureaucracy could ever hope to. Narratives composed by the poor describe losing jobs due to injury or mental illness, depict horrific tales of childhood abuse and spousal violence, recount the loss of friends and family members. They evoke the slipping away of social supports and government assistance, the descent into substance abuse and addiction, the harsh realities of life on the streets. These are the perspectives on poverty that are too often omitted from discussions over the extent of the problem and how to solve it.

Greenhaven Press's *Social Issues Firsthand* series provides a forum for the often-overlooked human perspectives on society's most divisive topics of debate. Each volume focuses on one social issue and presents a collection of ten to sixteen narratives by those who have had personal involvement with the topic. Extra care has been taken to include a diverse range of perspectives. For example, in the volume on adoption, readers will find the stories of birth parents who have made an adoption plan, adoptive parents, and adoptees themselves. After exposure to these varied points of view, the reader will have a clearer understanding that adoption is an intense, emotional experience full of joyous highs and painful lows for all concerned.

The debate surrounding embryonic stem cell research illustrates the moral and ethical pressure that the public brings to bear on the scientific community. However, while nonexperts often criticize scientists for not considering the potential negative impact of their work, ironically the public's reaction against such discoveries can produce harmful results as well. For example, although the outcry against embryonic stem cell research in the United States has resulted in fewer embryos being destroyed, those with Parkinson's, such as actor Michael J. Fox, have argued that prohibiting the development of new stem cell lines ultimately will prevent a timely cure for the disease that is killing Fox and thousands of others.

Each book in the series contains several features that enhance its usefulness, including an in-depth introduction, an annotated table of contents, bibliographies for further research, a list of organizations to contact, and a thorough index. These elements—combined with the poignant voices of people touched by tragedy and triumph—make the Social Issues Firsthand series a valuable resource for research on today's topics of political discussion.

Introduction

According to the United States Department of Justice, juvenile arrests have gone down 24 percent since 1997. The reason for this decline is debatable. Some suggest that the biggest factor is that more attention has been given to causes of juvenile crime, how to prevent it, and how to work with juveniles who have committed a crime. Proponents of this view maintain that such approaches can help juveniles avoid getting into the justice system—an important step, since the prognosis is bad for those who do end up incarcerated at a young age.

Prior to the 1900s, authorities in the United States dealt with juvenile crime by treating kids no differently from adults. Offenders over seven years old were jailed with adults. A few special jails for juveniles that were more focused on rehabilitation than punishment did exist, but they did not become common until the early 1900s. The first juvenile court opened in 1899.

The 1960s and early 1970s ushered in new, more juvenile-friendly laws, including ones that allocated more funding to juvenile delinquency programs and protected juvenile offenders by separating them from adult offenders. Starting in the 1990s, a "get tough on crime" attitude has taken over, and again, young offenders are being tried as adults. In some cases, children as young as ten have been tried as adults. As of this writing, in nineteen states, it was still legal to execute sixteen- and seventeen-year-olds for capital crimes.

While some credit the lower rates of juvenile crime to this new attitude, studies show that this is not necessarily the case. Researchers have found that juveniles who are incarcerated with adults rather than other juveniles have a higher likelihood of committing crimes again, and those who do reoffend tend to commit more violent crimes.

Critics of tougher sentencing instead link the drop in juvenile crime to prevention programs and alternative sentencing. They credit a more proactive approach: Rather than impose a harsh sentence on the offender, these newer techniques take a more long-term and holistic approach.

One technique championed by reformers is to offer help to first time, nonviolent offenders. Instead of being sent to juvenile court, where they face the possibility of jail time, the offenders take a class in which they learn about their crimes, complete a stint of community service, and work with their group on challenging projects. Such programs have been credited with steering juveniles away from crime and thus bringing down the rate of recidivism.

Other programs have been put in place to serve at-risk youth at an early age—even before they may commit a crime. Fresh Lifelines for Youth (FLY), a program in San Jose, California, was founded by juvenile offenders and works with at-risk and disadvantaged kids. The group offers a mentoring program, leadership training, and education about the law. Ten years after starting in 1998, the group claims an 85 percent success rate. Boys Hope Girls Hope, an organization based in Bridgeton, Missouri, offers a more comprehensive approach. The group serves children who are talented and motivated, but lack a supportive home environment. The children are placed in noninstitutional, family-style homes and into schools with rigorous academic requirements. The children are financially supported through college and, if necessary, beyond. At the same time, the parents remain involved with their children. Parents retain custody of their children and, if able, can participate in school events. Since 1991, 100 percent of the organization's U.S. high school graduates have gone on to college.

On a societal level, many experts now echo the idea expressed in the old adage that it "takes a village to raise a child." They suggest that when families are not providing a healthy or encouraging environment for a child, government and charitable organizations need to take over that role. In the past, such organizations offered only a patchwork of help, but families, government, and charitable groups are now learning to work together to offer a cohesive and effective support system to at-risk youth.

Programs to enhance parent education and participation are also recommended as a way to decrease juvenile crime. Studies show that men and women who take classes on parenting are more involved and better equipped to deal with their children. Offering a variety of programs has also been shown to increase participation. Some parents might not take a parenting class, but their child might be willing to get involved in an after-school program. Other programs such as sports leagues, support groups, homework help, and mental health counseling can be part of a menu of offerings that a community can make available to its youth.

It is clear that there is not a simple fix for juvenile crime, but that smart, steady, and consistent efforts among families, schools, and communities can make a big difference. In *Social Issues Firsthand: Juvenile Crime*, the authors provide personal narratives about their experiences with juvenile crime and juvenile criminals. Some authors describe their lives as juvenile criminals, while others write about offenders in their families or with whom they have worked. There are harrowing tales of growing up in unhappy homes, suffering from mental illness, and dealing drugs. Others write about suffering harsh punishments or being threatened at school. It becomes apparent from the accounts that juvenile crime touches more than just the offender and victim—it affects the whole society. And as a society, questions still remain about how to deal with, and prevent, juvenile crime.

SOCIAL ISSUES
FIRSTHAND

CHAPTER 1

Reasons for Turning to Crime

My Life as a Drug Dealer

Ariel Corporan as told to Stacy Abramson

The following selection is a transcript of a radio story about Ariel Corporan, a former juvenile inmate at Rikers Island, a large prison in New York City. In the story, Corporan tells of growing up on the streets and becoming a drug dealer. He weaves his reminiscences together with his interview of his mother. Corporan's story is part of a series called Youth Portraits. *The series came about when radio producer Stacy Abramson taught members of the Friends of the Island Academy how to use radio equipment to record their stories. The academy works with young people who have been in Rikers Island to help them avoid falling back into crime. About 70 percent of the young people released from Rikers return to jail, but among those particpating in academy programs, only 17 percent do.*

Host: Our first story is from Ariel Corporan. He was born in the Bronx and is now twenty-two years old. Ariel goes by the nickname Asun.

Ariel: Asun is like my alter ego I guess. It's this person who is cool with everybody in the streets, and everybody in the streets knows him.

I always felt like my family wasn't my family. I always felt like the outcast. I was always different.

As a little kid, I wouldn't want to come home. I would go to school. After school, I'll go to a park, then instead of taking a bus, I walk home, and it'll take me hours and hours to get home, and I loved it.

As far back as I can remember, I never felt close to my family. My dad left right after I was born, and my mom and I never understood each other. We're opposites in every way. She's very strict. I've always been more of a dreamer. She's probably the most serious person I know.

Ariel's Mother

Ariel's mother: Where's your questions?

Ariel: Describe me as a kid.

Ariel's mother: I have to answer this? When you were little . . . you were a good kid. You were quiet, and you did as you were told. I used to like to dress you up like a little man and show you off.

Ariel: I grew up in a rough neighborhood. My mom wanted to keep me out of trouble, so she made me stay in the house all the time. She was trying to protect me, but I felt trapped. Things got real bad when she married my stepfather. I was seven.

Ariel's mother: At that time it wasn't easy to find someone who was willing to take on all of that responsibility for somebody else's child.

Ariel: Did you guys discuss, like, the rules, regulations, or boundaries that, you know, he would have to, like, follow being a stepfather?

Ariel's mother: No.

Ariel: No. He had like total freedom?

Ariel's mother: No. He was your father. And your father wasn't around.

"A Prisoner in My Own House"

Ariel: When my stepfather moved in, I became a prisoner in my own house. At first I escaped into a fantasy world. I'd play hand-puppet games or lock myself in a bathroom and race cockroaches up the wall. But I got older. The more he kept me in, the more I wanted to leave. If I managed to escape, there were consequences.

Ariel's mother: His discipline got a little out of hand . . .

Ariel: Exactly. That's what I want to know. Did you guys ever talk about that?

Ariel's mother: What are you talking about? What do you mean did we talk? What did we talk about?

Ariel: Like, "Don't hit my kid so bad," or something. Did you ever say nothing?

Ariel's mother: There was one time when he beat you up very badly in the bathtub, and I talked to him because he got out of hand. But there's no list of rules and regulations. There's no, "Oh, hands off. That's my child. You can't touch him."

Ariel: But didn't you think that was harming me in any way?

Ariel's mother: That time when he beat you up like that? Yes.

Ariel: Oh, but I got beat up real bad.

Ariel's mother: He was disciplining you and punishing you and he was doing it for me. There were times when I felt that he was overly strict. But he was doing a job. He was doing the job of a father.

Ariel: Did it work?

Ariel's mother: Obviously not.

Rebellion

Ariel: I started to rebel. At home I was a nobody. I was alone, and I was weak. Outside of the house, I created a different me.

After my freshman year of high school I got locked up for smacking some kid and taking his book bag. I didn't even like the book bag, I just took it just to be a bad ass.

I was in Lincoln Hall. It's a juvenile facility called Lincoln Hall, in Lincolndale, New York. I learned from all these other juvenile delinquents how to be a delinquent, how to be a criminal, how to be a thug, how to be a drug dealer. By the time I got out of there I knew everything I needed to know about drugs: where to get them, where to push them, how to push them, where to stash them.

When I got back from juvenile detention, I started hustling. I was seventeen.

I was in school—in a high school called Truman High School—and I met this guy there in the cafeteria. His name was Harold. He told me to call him Biggs. He was a drug dealer. If you would have seen the roll of money this guy pulled out, you would have, like, melted. So of course I asked him about it. You know, "How can I get down? How can I get that kind of money?" And he said, "You could come work for me. We could make this money together. You can come to my block instead of going to school, and you could sell crack. You know how to sell crack?" I played it off like, "Yeah, I've hustled before, you know." I didn't know nothing. I didn't know nothing about the business. But I knew that I was determined to learn, and I was determined to be part of this inner circle, this forbidden family.

My First Day Hustling

I just started hustling. First day there, he was out there with me to let me know who the customers were. You know, like, "Sell to him, don't sell to him, sell to him, don't sell to him." And I was getting—I was getting pretty far. I was doing it good. Like the bundle was gone in less then an hour. That night I came home with about eighty bucks. And that was, like, my first time hustling. I was like, "Wow, I'm a drug dealer now."

I would leave my house at seven-thirty in the morning—to go to school supposedly. I'd be at the spot by nine. I was the hand-to-hand guy. I did the hand-to-hand sales, and I sold three-dollar bags, five-dollar bags, and somebody next to me sold the ten-dollar bags of dope.

After a few weeks, I got made a manager.

For a person like Biggs to give me authority, give me respect, to say, "Okay, I think you could handle this business right here." And for me to make money, and for me to meet people that think I'm cool—that was hot. I needed that.

You know how many times my mother told me I ain't shit, I ain't going to be shit? And I told her, "You know, I'm just leaving." You know? So I did it. I moved out. By the end of the night I had a room. By the end of the week, I had a whole apartment. At the age of seventeen.

My First Employee

My first employee was a guy named Kareem. He went by the name of Knowledge.

Knowledge and I became real tight. He was older than me, and I looked up to him.

He had like a funny beard, he had like a goat—it wasn't a goatee, because his mustache and his beard didn't connect yet. But his beard was like pointy and he had a funny mustache, and he had these eyes. His eyes was real. He could see right through you. He was twenty-one years old. He just came out of doing a five-year stretch, so he was real ganstafied, and he acted that way.

So Knowledge started coming to my house every morning. I would go under the mattress or under the rug where I had the crack stashed, pull out like three, four bundles, give him two and keep one on me. And I'd stay in front of the stoop talking to him a little bit until he starts getting customers. When customers start coming on the block, I'd send him around the corner. I'd stay in front of the building, where I am away from the crack and away from the crack dealing. And I'd just sit there.

I was tall. I had a nice little chain then. People started to recognize me. I looked different. I was a different face on block. They knew I was different there. They knew I had to be a hustler.

I Felt Invincible

I had it all. It was like a dream. I felt invincible.

Here it is: October 15, 1997. The year's almost over. I haven't been to school in a little while, and I'm almost out of crack.

Me and Knowledge was just kicking the breeze, and we sold a couple of slabs that were left, when this guy comes up to us and he's like, "Where's the crack out here?" He was short and stocky, and he was kind of well built for a crack head. He was clean cut, which is not the norm. I looked at Knowledge, and Knowledge already knew. He was like "No, I don't sell crack. Go down the block."

The dude's like, "No, you all sell crack. Let me get two slabs. I know you got slabs." Now, we call crack "slabs." Crack heads come, "Let me get a hit. Let me get two hits." They don't say slabs; we say slabs. And Knowledge was telling the guy, "Look, we don't sell crack, B." This guy was insisting too, like, "I know you sell crack. Just give me my two slabs," even though we told him no like three thousand times. And Knowledge was like, "Look, man, I don't sell crack. Get off my block talking all that nonsense." The guy sits down on the stoop a couple of feet away from us, so I moved over a little bit. And I saw them arguing. And they go at it. And the dude is on Knowledge. And Knowledge got him in a full nelson, and he's trying to reach for his gun. So when he went to reach for his gun, I reached for his gun, too. I reached for his hand. His hand clutched the gun. He was pulling it out. When I seen him pulling it out, I pushed it in. I think when I pushed it in, that's when it went off.

When that gun shot went off, in the blink of a second a whole bunch of other cops started shooting at us out of nowhere.

Gunfire and Chaos

Two vans pulled up. A car and a fat guy with a gun that was right there on the corner, shooting at me. I mean right, right in front of me, shooting directly at me. I saw the smoke coming out that barrel.

I saw the gun. I just saw the gun. I saw holes of the revolver around the barrel. I saw his hand clutching the trigger.

I saw his white fingers. It seemed like something out of a Bruce Willis movie. He was just running at me, shooting at me.

And I got shot in my leg. It felt cold. And then I felt my hot blood on my skin, which was getting numb. Then I got shot again. And I kept my hands up: "I'm hit. You shot me. I'm shot!" So some cop comes up to me, puts handcuffs on me, and drags me to the corner. And they were still shooting. They were shooting at Knowledge.

When I turned around, I saw Knowledge, and Knowledge was bleeding out his neck. And Kareem looked up at me, and he was crying. He was saying he can't breathe. "Hey, Asun, I can't breathe. I can't breathe. I'm ain't going to make it." He was dying—he was dying, and he was telling me he was dying.

One hundred and seventy-two shells were recovered. No weapons or drugs were found, and I was sent to jail anyway. My lawyer told me to plead guilty to armed robbery and assualt to avoid trial.

Home Again

When I came home from Rikers, I'd lost the apartment I was living in, my clothes were in bags, and I had no money. But it didn't matter anymore. The incident had changed me. This tough drug-dealing character I'd created for myself died the minute Knowledge did. I was ready to just be me, even with my mom.

My stepfather's not around anymore, but my mom's just as hard on me as she ever was, especially about the incident.

Ariel's mother: It would upset me tremendously to hear you talk about it as if it was somebody else's fault. Yes, they shot at you from behind. But you were not supposed to be there.

Ariel: Do you feel lucky?

Ariel's mother: *You* should feel lucky that you're alive.

Ariel: I have three jobs now. I have a girlfriend I'm about to marry and a beautiful seven-month-old baby boy. And me and my mom? We'll keep working on it.

Ariel's mother: I got to go to sleep.

Ariel: I still got to ask you more questions.

Ariel's mother: But I got to go to sleep. I'm sorry, its one o'clock in the morning, and I got to go to sleep.

Ariel: Can we finish this some other day?

Ariel's mother: Some other day, but I got to go to sleep.

Ariel: Cool.

Host: Ariel lives with his girlfriend, Leilani, and their ten-month-old son, Dei-Jean, in Brooklyn. He works for an outreach coordinator on Rikers Island.

Foster Care, Mental Health Facilities, and the Juvenile Justice System

Roger Weisberg and Vanessa Roth

The following selection is the transcript of an interview with David Griffin about his life in foster care, mental health facilities, and the juvenile justice system. Griffin was taken from his mother when he was less than a year old after his mother was diagnosed with chronic paranoid schizophrenia. Griffin was quickly found a foster home, but was unable to stay when his foster parents could not handle his violent outbursts and emotional problems. It was a cycle that would repeat itself. Griffin entered group homes, juvenile detention centers, and drug treatment programs but was unable to find the help that would allow him to lead a normal life. Griffin's story is part of Aging Out, *a film by Roger Weisberg and Vanessa Roth about aging out of the foster care system that aired on public television.*

David Griffin spent virtually his entire childhood in the foster care, mental health, and juvenile justice systems. David was taken from his mother when he was less than a year old. She was diagnosed with chronic paranoid schizophrenia and deemed unable to care for him. Both David and his sister, Sherilyn, were sent to the home of Bob and Pearl Galasso.

The Galassos were very keen to keep the siblings together. However, David's severe emotional problems eventually overwhelmed the family. He was out of control and was often violent with the other children and his foster mother, Pearl. At age five, the Galassos had to let David go. However, they told him he was always welcome back, and he would return to visit and stay with them at various times in the future.

David: I never grew up with a mother and father. I had like 30 mothers and fathers. I was nine years old when I went to my first group home. That's when I really started getting in trouble. While I was there, I committed five crimes and I was sent to ju-vie [the juvenile detention center] four times. I've had therapists since I was three years old, which gives me like a doctor's degree in therapy. They tried to diagnose me with Tourette's [syndrome], bipolar, manic depressive. They tried to say I had ADD [attention deficit disorder], ADHD [attention deficit hyperactivity disorder], everything.

Twenty Foster Care Placements

David turned 18 when he was in his 20th foster care placement, a group home called Journey House. Although most teens emancipate from the foster care system at age 18, David was required to remain at Journey House for six more months. He had recently been incarcerated for burglary and, as a condition of his release, had to stay in foster care until he completed high school. However, Tim Mayworm, the group home's director, grew fed up with David's behavior and decided he had to go. "I just decided that David stopped growing," says Mayworm. "His capacity to learn was over. He just couldn't listen to anybody, he just couldn't talk anymore. Nothing we were doing was working. So, I just said 'You're going to have to leave here.'" David left the home and he began using drugs and committing petty crime.

Tim wanted me to get my high school diploma. His cause was righteous you know, but I ditched every day at school all day long. I would just go get high. I'm a true addict.

They kicked me out. So I grabbed my stuff and at the time I was despairing. Where am I going to go? What am I going to do? I'm going to be a bum on the streets. I was staying at this dude's house. He lived in the garage and we did a lot of drugs for about two and a half weeks, to the point where I didn't go to sleep for like four days straight once. During that four days I had one bowl of Captain Crunch, that was it.

"Broke and Homeless"

One part of me was totally happy and exhilarated because I was free. Another part of me was full of despair because I was broke and homeless. I burglarized some dude's house. I came up on like $500. Then we just spent it all on drugs and Burger King.

When he could no longer find a place to sleep, David went to the home of the Galassos. He tried to convince Bob and Pearl to let him stay with them. Instead, they convinced him to turn himself into the juvenile authorities. Because he had gone AWOL [absent without leave] from the system, there was a warrant for David's arrest.

I've known these foster parents since I was a little kid, so they are like a second family. I tried to convince them to actually let me live with them again, but they ended up convincing me to turn myself in. They said, "You know, just do it right." I walked in the station and I said, "I am David Griffin. There's a warrant for my arrest and I'm turning myself in." It was the hardest thing to do and I totally regret it. I wish I didn't do it.

After spending two months locked up in Juvenile Hall, David was discharged to another group home. Soon after his arrival, he ran away again and went back to the Galassos. This time they agreed to let him stay with them for a while. David had been living at their home for two months when he was stopped by a police officer in his neighborhood. The officer discovered David's outstanding warrant for going AWOL from his last group home. The officer arrested David and, because he was 18, transferred him to a county jail.

Released from Jail

I thought I was going to do about two years in jail, but I didn't even go to court. The deputy walks in and tells me that I've been released off of probation and I am no longer a ward of the court.

Because David was 18 and his only offense was going AWOL from his group home placements, a judge decided to close his case and remove him from the authority of the juvenile system. His case closed, David tried to enroll in the military. He was turned down because of his psychiatric record. David began disappearing for days at a time. Suspecting that he was using drugs, the Galassos reached their limit and asked him to leave. They persuaded him to go to an independent living program. He agreed, but later balked when he realized it was also a drug treatment program.

When I got to Lancaster, I was all pissed because it was a freakin' behavioral treatment center and I thought I was going to my own apartment. I'm like "You guys can drug test me all you want, I'm not going to no damn freakin' drug treatment though." It's still part of the system, that's why and I have rules that I have to abide by. I really don't have a plan but I want to travel as much as I possibly can. I want to go to Easter Island, visit the pyramids at Giza, go to Japan, become a full time ninja. I always got to be on the move. Always.

After only two weeks at the independent living facility, David was suspected of vandalizing a nearby school and went AWOL again. With another warrant out for his arrest, David headed to his friend's house in the desert, but he did not plan on staying long.

Hoping for a New Life

I'm going to start a new life. I decided that I needed to leave. I'm going to go up to Alaska. People don't know who I am. They don't know a single thing about me. That's for the better, because I want to start a new life. That's exactly what I plan on doing, because you know I've been screwing up left and right. It's tiring. It's an opportunity and it's desperation on my part.

What I see happening to me in the future is either being on the streets or going to jail, because I'm wanted in the city and because all the people I know out here are just stoners and drug users. That's exactly what I am, and I don't want to be that. I'm not going to go up there with any money because I don't have any money. I want to make a life that I can call a life, something that I can be at least a little bit proud of. I'm definitely not proud of my life right now. The only thing I'm proud about is my defiance that I've held on to for so many years, but that gets old. The only way that I'm going to make it is if I do it on my own.

Epilogue

After traveling by bus to Seattle on his way to Alaska, David was unable to find a job on a fishing boat. He spent a year living on the streets of Seattle, receiving occasional services from a drop-in center for homeless youth where he went to shower and have occasional meals. He is now hitchiking across the country. The Galassos, his foster family, are in regular contact with him.

I Was a Gang Member

Yovani Whyte as told to Stacy Abramson

The following selection is from a transcript of a radio series titled Youth Portraits *that documents the lives of juvenile offenders who have done time at New York's Rikers Island prison. In this selection Yovani Whyte describes her life as a teenage member of the Bloods gang in Crown Heights, Brooklyn. She interviews her friends and family and explains why she decided to join the gang and describes some of her criminal activities. Whyte is currently studying fashion at the New York City Technical College.*

Host: Now a story from Yovani Whyte. She's twenty years old and grew up in Crown Heights, Brooklyn. Today, she attends the New York City Technical College. As a teenager she was a gang member.

Yovani: When I was sixteen, I was initiated into the Bloods. I wore a lot of red. I wouldn't wear a outfit if it didn't have something red in it. As long as I had something red on, it was okay.

Every morning I'd punch in at school and leave. Then me and my friends would figure out what we were gonna do for the day. If we felt like chilling, we'd chill. If we felt like robbing someone, we'd just do that too.

All you needed to say was, "I'm starting it." And the starter would just go up to the person and be like, "Give me your jewelry." And if the person don't give up their jewelry, the rest of us get involved. But the starter normally just takes it how she wants it. If she wants to just haul off and hit the girl, or just haul off and say give me your jewelry, or just snatch it from her, that's her decision. We just there to back her up.

My Younger Brother

Hello, I am talking with Eduardo Whyte, my brother. What's your age and what's your relation to me?

Eduardo: My name is Eduardo Whyte. I'm eighteen, and this is my sister, Yovani Whyte.

Yovani: Okay, Eduardo, this tape is about my life, mostly around the age seventeen. Can you tell me what you think about it?

Eduardo: Messed up. Where do you want me to begin?

Yovani: What was the worse thing I ever did?

Eduardo: Damn, you did a lot of bad shit.

Yovani: What do you think about me being Blood?

Eduardo: It's good to me.

Yovani: Do you remember the first time that I told you I was turning Blood?

Eduardo: Yeah.

Yovani: What happened?

Eduardo: I was like, "Well, good," because I was planning on being Blood anyway, so I decided since she was gonna do it, I was gonna do it.

Yovani: I started getting a record when I was fourteen for little stuff, misdemeanors. Then when I hit sixteen: robbery. Then I kept robbing people, kept doing a whole bunch of things I shouldn't have been doing. And when I was seventeen, me and this girl cut this girl in my school, and they locked me up.

I remember the day after very clearly, because I went to school and I couldn't go to none of my classes. It took like eight people to try to sneak me out of school because cops was all in my school—they were searching for me everywhere. And then they came to my house like a week later and got me.

My mom bailed me out. She wasn't too mad. She would have done the same thing back in her day. My family loves to fight. . . .

My Mother

Growing up, there were two women in my life. My grand-mother, who I loved. She raised me, she was everything to me. Then there was my mother. She was always hard on me. So look what happened; I turned out hard too. . . .

I heard when my mom was seventeen, she was just like me. She was violent. I don't know what weapons she used, but I used razor blades. I used to sneak them into school.

The little ones that's rectangularish, they come with like an envelope. You can have it undone and put it like in the gums of your mouth, down so the metal detector ring but when they're searching you, they not going to put the metal detector over your mouth. So you can put it down in your gum, but you had to be careful with that, because if nobody knows you have a razor, they hit you and you would bust your whole mouth. It just rip you open. But that's the best thing, because if you know how to carry it and you can talk regular with it in your mouth, they won't know—somebody will think you just fighting and then you throw your hand, you just spit the razor right out into your hand and you cut them and they won't know what happened.

Everybody have to go through something to get accepted. You don't just turn Blood and be like, "Okay, you Blood, that's it." You have to get accepted everywhere you go, into every neighborhood you go. The neighborhood has to accept you. So you always proving yourself, showing that you can take care of yourself, you bad, you can stand on your own two feet, you can hold it down, whatever.

Why Did I Get into Trouble?

(To Eduardo) Why do you think that I first got into trouble?

Eduardo: Because you was born.

Yovani: Shut up.

Interviewing my brother Eduardo again.

Why do you think I first got into trouble? Do you even know? Do you even think about it?

Eduardo: Because of following the wrong crowd.

Yovani: Do you remember Maria and Daniella?

Eduardo: Oh, Murder One and Murder Two? Yeah, because they always followed my sister. Everything she did, they did.

Maria: Hello, my name is Maria, and I am seventeen, and—oh, and this is my sister.

Daniella: Hello, my name is Daniella, I'm nineteen.

Maria: We live in Crown Heights and we went to Prospect Heights High School. When Yovani came to school, we just clicked and became good friends and robbing buddies.

Daniella: We started talking and we just got along right on that spot.

Yovani: Maria and Daniella were Blood like me. But some of the older Bloods thought they weren't tough enough. So one day they made Maria and Daniella prove themselves by doing a robbery.

Maria: I didn't think nothing of it because I'm always robbing somebody, so I just really didn't give a f[---]. I just wanted to get it over with. And I remember they sent Yovani to the park to wait for us. A boy named Black, he gave me a blade and I took it from him, then, you know, they pointed to the person who they wanted us to rob.

Daniella: Well, actually, I approached the girl and I was like, "Give me your stuff." She was like, "What?" I started attacking her.

Yovani: Maria went to hit the girl, and forgot she had the blade in her hand.

Maria: I looked back up to see the girl I cut bleeding and holding her neck.

Daniella: My sister and I, we just looked and ran.

Maria: And basically, I got caught like five days later.

My Best Friends in Jail

Yovani: Maria and Daniella got locked up. They were my best friends, so I had to look after them no matter what, even if it meant going back to jail. Remember that cutting I did at my school? I never showed up at the trial, so there was already a warrant out for my arrest. I turned myself in. I was on Rikers Island for a year.

Ricky: My name is Ricky, and I'm your brother. My dad and your mom are girlfriend and boyfriend, I guess. Don't know what they are, but they are confused too, so . . .

Yovani: How long they been together?

Ricky: Since as long as I can remember. I'm thirteen years old, so that's pretty long.

Yovani: Do you remember anything that mommy or your father used to say when I went to jail?

Ricky: They didn't say nothing. They just forgot all about you.

Yovani: Well, then how did you find out I was in jail?

Ricky: I asked my father, "Where was Yovani?" and he said, "Yovani is in jail." We never said anything else about it.

Yovani: Damn. So they didn't mention me?

Ricky: No, not really. Not that I can remember.

Yovani: Well, you're young and stupid.

When I came home I was really lonely. People was dead, locked up. I didn't have no more friends. Everybody I knew was dead or in jail. And I guess if I wouldn't have been in there, I'd have been dead too. When Maria and Daniella got locked up, Maria had a baby that was one. When she got out, he was three.

(To Maria) What do you think about being Blood or when you was Blood?

Maria: Well, at first I thought it was, you know, real fun. Maybe I just wanted to fit in. But my ways just changed, because I know that being Blood got me into a lot of trouble.

Daniella: Half of the stuff all of us were doing, we don't do anymore.

Maria: I don't know. I don't want to go back to doing the same stuff I was doing just to be known or whatever.

Brother Following the Same Path

Yovani: Now Maria and Daniella stay out of trouble. But my brother Eduardo? He's still Blood, still thinking he's gangster, trying to act like I used to act.

(To Eduardo) Why did you look up to me?

Eduardo: I guess because you was older and doing dumb shit, and I thought it was cool.

Yovani: You looked up to me because I used to do dumb shit?

Eduardo: We was kids back then. Come on now. What do you expect?

Yovani: Do you still look up to me?

Eduardo: No.

Yovani: Why not?

Eduardo: You're not keeping it gangster!

He's right. I'm not looking to rob nobody anymore, or cut them. I'm in college now. Maybe someday Eduardo will follow me there too. You might be wondering what changed. Partly I just grew up. But mostly it was my grandmother. She was everything to me. And she died while I was locked up.

What Changed Me

When she got real sick, she started asking for me. My family told her I was away. When I finally found out, I wrote her a letter. But by the time it got to the hospital, my grandmother was already dead.

I was so upset, I tried to kill myself. But then I thought, "No, I'm just going to show her." Now I'm doing everything she wanted me to do before she died. She wanted me to go to school, now I'm in school. She wanted me to get a job, now I got a job. And I think that maybe she even would have wanted me to make this story.

This is for you grandma.

I'm Yovani Whyte.

Host: Yovani lives in Flatbush, Brooklyn. She attends New York City Technical College where she's studying fashion marketing.

My Life in Crime: Four Young People Speak Out

Mark Johnson

In the following selection, four British teenagers—Joe, fifteen; Germain, eighteen; Helen, seventeen; and Steffi, fifteen—describe their lives in crime and offer their thoughts on how—and whether—they might have been deterred from such a life. Despite their different crimes and situations, all four teens note that boredom played a large role in leading them into crime.

Joe, 15

In the past few years I've been in five care homes. It's because I'm always in trouble and they can't deal with me. So that's what "care" means to me: moving about.

I used to live with my dad. He doesn't really care. When I was in trouble and had to go home, I'd stand at the door not wanting to ring the bell. Ding-dong. He'd throw down the keys and it was like getting hit by a bomb. Then I'd rush into the bedroom quick and I'd think, "Don't come in, don't come in." But he always came in and I'd get the shit knocked out of me. I got used to it after a while. It was: here we go again.

I've been in so much trouble it's unreal. [Arrested for committing the crimes of] GBH [grievous bodily harm], ABH [actual bodily harm], knives, assault, public disorder . . . most of my arrests are for fighting. I mean, it's impossible to catch me for shoplifting. A security guard did once try to grab me, he hit me. I went back with all my mates [friends] from the estate [public housing project] and we really beat him up. I said to him: "That's what you get when you play with big boys." He must have been pissed off, a big security guard lying on the floor because he's been beaten up by a load of 12-year-olds.

A lot of the fighting I do is caused by boredom. And the excitement of being in a gang. When I was at primary school we waited at the gates of another school with the parents and at 3.30PM they opened the gates and we ran in and battered the kids. I took it more seriously than the others; I was out to hurt them more. Probably it came from watching films: you see it on a film and you want to do it yourself.

It's impossible for the government to change things unless they stick officers on every street corner and we know they can't do that. They can't stop people getting beaten up as they'd be beaten up themselves, and back-up wouldn't arrive in time. It might help if there was more to do. If you're playing basketball or football, you're not out fighting, are you?

Germain, 18

I was a bright kid in primary school and didn't get into any trouble, but I had an unlucky start with my family. My dad went off, my mother had a new husband and I had lots of little brothers and sisters. From the ages of about seven to 10 there were fights all the time. My mother, my stepfather, my brother, me. The police used to come, sometimes three times a day. I'd cry myself to sleep every night, covered in blood, listening to the rats. My mother was running around a lot, I don't judge her for this. I think she was into class A's [drugs]. So she'd go off for two weeks, no food in the house. I was in charge, changing nappies [diapers], getting kids to school. My first arrest was for stealing a tin of SMA Gold baby milk.

At secondary school, I was arrested almost every day. I started with the Bob Marley [marijuana] and began running away. I was in a gang and we'd go everywhere, down to the south coast, robbing shops, people on buses. Sometimes just a few of us, sometimes 30. I was a gang leader and if anyone attacked a gang member . . . well, I remember this kid. I was told he was 19 but I beat him up really bad; he was in hospital. When I looked at him I saw he was just 16 or 17.

I don't carry a knife now but I still sleep with one under my pillow. But forget the robberies, the shoplifting, the fights—the worst thing I did was this kidnapping. I was feeling bored, no, angry, and there was this kid ... well, what I did was sick and gruesome and I don't want to talk about it any more.

I was saved by an organisation called Kids Company where I go and they listen to me and help me. They're like my family. That's what's worked for me. Not the law, not the police, who just want to lock you up. I haven't committed a crime for two years and it's because of the support I've had.

Helen, 17

I come from an estate in the Midlands where everyone's related. I hung around with my generation, who were all older than me. We were close, but there was infighting between the families: once, my Dad got stabbed for beating up the family that beat up my brother.

Dad couldn't work because of an industrial accident and for years money was tight because we were waiting for the compensation. When I was young my parents were on base [amphetamines]; there were loads of parties downstairs. Then someone died on coke and the parties stopped.

My first arrest was when some bigger kids hot-wired a car. I had to pretend I'd been driving it because I was 12 and wouldn't go to jail. After that, because I was small and skinny, they used me for burglaries—I'd fit through top windows.

I did really well at school until the end of term, when we had time off for exams. I was so lonely and bored I couldn't stand it. I started a relationship with a boy who used heroin and began to smoke it myself. I loved it. Straight to oblivion. I was so sick of my parents hassling me to get a job, so sick of worrying my boyfriend would cheat on me. I smoked every day for three days and after that the rattle [withdrawal symptoms] was so bad I'd commit any crime to get money for more. I worked at McDonald's and stole from the till; I scared people at cash machines; when my Dad's compensation came through I used his bank card to gradually steal about £20,000 before he realised; the worst crime was, when an old lady fell over bleeding in the street, I ran off with her purse.

I'm in rehab now and I feel so bad about everything I did, so guilty about hurting my parents. Looking back, I think a bit of drug education might have helped. If I'd known more . . .

Most of our crime was controlled by an older lad. We were scared of him and all did exactly what he said, even though he was grassing us up [reporting us] to the police. Because he grassed, the police gave him an easy ride, although he was really at the root of it. The police were useless on our estate, there was no point them being there, same goes for the YOT [Youth Offending Teams] worker, the Asbo [Anti-Social Behaviour Order, an order given to a person for anti-social behavior], everything.

I was one of a huge gang of kids on the estate and the path to crime for us was definitely not having anything else to do; the one way the government could cut down on drug use and street crime would be giving us something else do to.

Steffi, 15

I live in south London. My family's OK, that's not the problem, the problem is the other people in our neighbourhood. I've been robbed and beaten up so many times.

I first smoked weed when I was 11. It made me sick. I've smoked it every day since. They found weed on me when I was 13 and I was excluded from school. It was their zero-tolerance policy. But they didn't find me another school.

I've only robbed one person, when I was 13. My parents don't have any money to buy me clothes or a phone and there was this girl with a nice phone, money, jewellery. So I went up to her and patted her down and took her phone. Afterwards I felt quite bad. I wanted to give it back. I'm a nice girl. But I did do one other thing which wasn't very nice. I was a bit depressed at the time and I saw this young girl and thought, "She looks so happy, she's rich, she's got everything she wants, she's still in school." I wanted just to destroy her face a little bit and I really punched her; her face was bad.

On the streets these days everyone's a challenger. I usually carry a knife because if you look at a certain person in a certain way, that could be your life ended. If you show fear, if you don't act hard, they'll take advantage of you. It's all about respect. Recently a gang of black kids on the bus took my phone and really beat me up. All because I was sitting by myself, a little black girl with my hair straightened, listening to my music and they thought, "She looks innocent, she looks like a victim."

As for the law, I don't think people can make laws for kids unless they get involved with us. If there was a choice of activities I'd follow something else but there's only one activity, and that's drugs, so I followed it.

To be honest, I am a bored young woman but I have a lively mind. I like to dance, I'm very artistic and I like poetry, art; I love drawing, music, writing songs. But I've been excluded from school so how am I ever going to learn the big words the government uses so I can talk to them?

SOCIAL ISSUES
FIRSTHAND

CHAPTER 2

Punishments and Other Consequences

Doing Time in Los Angeles Day Camps

L.A. Youth

The following selection features interviews with five teens who were placed in Los Angeles County's "day camps." The day camps are a type of penal institution where youths serve time after committing a crime. The teens describe their experience in the camps and discuss whether or not the camps are a good idea. Although several describe bad experiences in the camps, ranging from simply being bored to being pulled out of bed and forced to march, they agree that it is better than the alternative—youth prison.

L A. County might close its 19 youth "day camps" because of state budget cuts. A day camp is not a boot camp or a summer camp—it's a type of jail where youth serve time after they're convicted of a crime. It's worse than being on house arrest or being in a group home placement, but not as bad as being in the California Youth Authority, the youth prisons where more serious offenders are housed.

L.A. Youth asked . . . teens who had been in the camps: Should the camps be shut down? They said no. Even though they felt the camps didn't help them, the camps were safer and less strict than a youth prison or juvenile hall.

M.N., A 16-year-old female from the San Gabriel Valley

What did you do that first got you into the juvenile justice system?

When I was 12, I was harassed by the police for doing what I loved most, skateboarding and being Mexican. I got a

L.A. Youth, "Should the Camps Be Closed?" May-June 2008. Reproduced by permission.

ticket for skateboarding on the sidewalk. At age 14 I was arrested for possession of a gun, methamphetamines possession, evading police and giving false information.

Have you ever spent time in the day camps?

Yes. I spent seven months at Camp Joseph Scott in Saugus.

What was your experience like in the day camps?

I had horrible experiences. I hated it. It got me more angry and it didn't help me with anything. It actually taught me to be a better criminal. My experiences were really bad. Like take this for example. Nine P.M. in the dorm (where all the girls sleep) was "off the hook." Girls were being loud, gangbanging. Some of us were trying to sleep. The staff lined us up, made us put on our boots and just our nightgowns. We went outside and all of us marched around the track. Then we had to stop, do 100 jumping jacks, then march again. We did this like five times around the track. Then we went back inside. We were all cold. I was mad. There weren't a lot of positive things. I can actually count them on my fingers. They had mentors. My mentor helped me a lot. There was church every Sunday.

Do you think the day camps should be closed?

No, because camps are one step away from Y.A. [California Youth Authority, the youth prisons]. And if they do, then everybody, like me, would go to Y.A.

What are your future goals?

To go to college and do something with animals 'cause I wanna make a difference in their life.

Do you consider yourself a bad kid?

No, I don't consider myself a "bad kid." I consider myself misunderstood and unique in my own ways. I just have to follow the "laws."

K.J., A 16-year-old male from Compton

What did you do that first got you into the juvenile justice system?

I went outside one day and I saw my homies. I walked over to them, and all of a sudden the cops pulled up and arrested us and took us to the station. That's where I learned that my homies had robbed two people that day. They still had all the stuff in their bags. Even though I wasn't even there, I was charged with robbery with a deadly weapon.

Have you ever spent time in the day camps?

Camp Miller [in Malibu] for four months.

What was your experience like in the day camps?

I was treated bad. Some people showed me love, but most of them didn't.

Do you think the day camps should be closed?

No. If there was no camps, I would've gone to Y.A. I heard that they are raping people, killing people in the Y.A. At least they don't kill nobody in the camps.

What are your future goals?

To stay out of jail, get on with my life, get a job.

Do you consider yourself a bad kid?

No, I'm just a kid that made a bad mistake and got busted. People who do crimes that don't get busted are labeled good so I'm not bad. I'm like everyone else.

D.C., a 17-year-old male from Los Angeles

What did you do that first got you into the juvenile justice system?

Possession of a firearm.

Have you ever spent time in the day camps?

I was at Camp Holton [in San Fernando] for four months, then at Camp Smith [in Lancaster] for four months, then Camp Paige [in La Verne] for nine months.

What was your experience like in the day camps?

It was very boring and it does not teach you anything. It is just stressful and a waste of time because nobody seems to care and a lot of people get blamed for things they didn't do.

Do you think the day camps should be closed?

No, because more kids will go to prison or Y.A.

What are your future goals?

To graduate from high school and go to college.

Do you consider yourself a bad kid?

No, I do not consider myself a bad kid. I just hang around bad people.

D.U., a 17-year-old male from South Central L.A.

What did you do that first got you into the juvenile justice system?

Making a terrorist threat when I was 12. I told my momma I was gonna kill her.

Have you ever spent time in the day camps?

Three months at Camp Smith [in Lancaster] and nine months at Camp Jarvis [in Lancaster].

What was your experience like in the day camps?

Stressing. I was thinking about going home. The people around you mess up and it makes the program go slower. There's stupid kids in camp. They're always playing, always talking mess to a person way bigger than them when they know the staff is right there. In order for them to get right the staff takes it out on us.

It was never boring. You wake up at 6:45, make your heads [bathroom] calls that last till 7:45. Then we'll go eat breakfast. From then on until the time to go to school we kick it, watch TV or something. School was cool because you can do anything you want, the computer, the Internet. Then we go back to the unit and just kick it. It's a privilege to do a chore, to clean the hallway or something. You get extra points on the merit ladder. There are 51 people and the top 10 get the jobs. The RL (run leader) runs the whole dorm. The XO (executive officer) is second down from the RL. The UL is the unit leader. The QM (quarter master) takes care of clothes. There's also four KPs (kitchen person), two dorm orderlies (DO) which switch off every week and get to stay up until 10 o'clock, and one librarian. I had all these jobs. It took me a while though. In camp all I'd do was fight and fight with enemies, people talking stuff.

Do you think the day camps should be closed?

Yes, so instead of going to camp, they'd go to placements first. In placements you have better privileges, like you get to wear your own clothes just like at home.

What are your future goals?

Go to college.

Do you consider yourself a bad kid?

Yep, I'm dangerous. . . .

R.A., a 17-year-old female from the San Fernando Valley

What did you do that first got you into the juvenile justice system?

Driving without owner's consent at age 13 (I borrowed my mom's car).

Have you ever spent time in the day camps?

Yes, Camp Onizuka [in Lancaster] for two months.

What was your experience like in the day camps?

It was really bad. I wasn't really ready to change so I made it my interest to break all the rules and get kicked out. They made us wake up so early. If we were bad the day before they would wake us up like at 4:30 in the morning to go marching around the facility. The worst part for me was having the other minors telling you what to do. They would have what we call XO's and RL's, meaning they were the minors who were in charge, kind of like the staff. The regular staff were just kind of like their backup.

Do you think the day camps should be closed?

In a way I do and in a way I don't. I feel they should because they really don't help youth, but then again I [don't] because they would only have two places to send troubled youth, Juvenile Hall or CYA.

What are your future goals?

I plan to get certified as a cosmetologist and open a beauty shop.

Do you consider yourself a bad kid?

No, I consider myself a child that needed help to bloom into the beautiful person that I know I am.

My Son Got Help, Not Jail

The following essay was written by an anonymous mother whose son was caught shoplifting while they were together on a family shopping trip. She was shocked—her son was an honor roll student and involved with extracurricular activities. She feared that her son would be sent to jail, but instead, her son was offered a space in a special program for nonviolent offenders. In the program, her son did community service work, wrote a research paper on his crime, and worked with his group on mental and physical challenges. He learned where crime could lead, saw how his behavior was affecting others, and learned positive things he was capable of achieving. "To me," the mother writes, "this was a much better way to deal with a problem."

As I left the local discount store with my daughter, age 12 and two sons, ages three and 14, a young man wearing the store uniform approached me at the exit doors.

"Ma'am, I'd like to talk with you about some merchandise that your son shoplifted."

My initial reaction was numbness, followed by a sickening feeling of doom and a lump of fear in my throat. I looked at him blankly, and replied in confusion, "I don't know what you mean."

"I know you don't," he said. "Let's step inside and I'll explain."

A jumble of thoughts flooded my mind during the short walk to the security office. This couldn't be real; it was all some sort of mix-up. My teenaged son looked as if he had no idea what was going on. Could he be talking about my three-year-old? Maybe he had picked something up and I had acci-

Anonymous, "Second Chances," *Connect for Kids*, March 3, 2007. Reproduced by permission.

dentally gone through checkout without noticing? But it was for real—and it was serious. Within minutes, I was viewing security camera videotape of my fourteen-year-old son shoplifting. Shocked and embarrassed beyond belief, I could hardly stand to watch. It was a mother's nightmare.

This was the beginning of an ordeal I never dreamed I'd experience. Though my son had gone through his share of normal teenage difficulties, he was a good kid who rarely went against the grain. An honor roll student, who kept busy with extracurricular activities, I couldn't believe he was capable of theft. But now I had to face reality. Any kid, even my own, can struggle with the temptation to steal.

Waiting for Punishment

Two excruciating hours later, we left the shopping center. My son had just experienced what it feels like to be a criminal, and I had witnessed it all. He endured the questioning of two security guards and a rightfully disgruntled police officer, not to mention his mother's hurt and angry looks. He was photographed along with his stolen loot, a thirty-dollar video game accessory, and sent home with a summons to appear in court and a juvenile arrest record. Had I not been with him that day, he would have been taken to jail.

Of course he was punished at home and endured the next month with no video games, phone calls or visits with friends. He never dared complain, he knew he deserved that and more. Weeks passed as we waited for the dreaded call, notifying us of his court date, and I began to wonder how long this would be hanging over our heads.

But before that call ever came, we received a letter from Neighborhood Youth Services, a community program that focuses on strengthening families and preventing delinquency. My son was selected to take part in their Youth Diversion Program—if we were interested. It was an answer to my prayers.

An Alternative to Court

The Youth Diversion Program is for first offenders of non-violent crimes, funded by our local United Way. Through thirty hours of community service, group meetings and asset-building exercises, participants are given a second chance at a clean record. I registered my son immediately and he started the program the following week.

There were eight kids in my son's group. They were a diverse group of kids, there for everything from theft to curfew violations. Over the next three weeks, the group would accomplish sixteen hours of community service work, including clean-up projects and a nursing home visit. They would attend group meetings, where they would do such projects as writing an apology letter and a research paper on their crime. They would also face mental and physical challenges presented through activities like rock climbing and group problem solving. It was a lot to accomplish in thirty hours' time.

At the program's end, everyone took part in a "graduation ceremony." The parents were invited to the community center, where the kids were presented with a certificate of completion. As they received their certificates, the adult leader told us something positive that he had learned about each child. Though they were a bit embarrassed by the attention, you could see the pride of accomplishment in their faces.

The Road Less Traveled

Perhaps if we had chosen to take our son to court, the experience would have frightened and humiliated him enough to prevent further criminal behavior. But to me, this was a much better way to deal with a problem. These kids weren't coddled, they worked hard and paid their dues, but they gained so much more. They saw where a life of crime could lead. They saw how their behavior has an effect on others. They saw what they were capable of, by testing their mental and physical strengths.

We were surprised to find that many parents who are offered this program turn down the opportunity. Perhaps they feel that the court system will be a more effective punishment for their child, but the Diversion Program's record speaks for itself. Their success rates for preventing second offenses is right around 85 percent, as opposed to juvenile court's rate of approximately 45 percent.

I never thought that something like this would happen in my family. We've done our best to teach our children right from wrong and tried to provide a good example to our kids. But the reality is that even good kids can give in to temptation in a weak moment. The importance of talking about tough issues can't be stressed enough, no matter how uncomfortable it may be. Temptation is there and it is real—no family is immune.

I've also gained a new appreciation for community programs for kids and the volunteers who care enough to give of themselves and their time. Prior to this happening in our lives, we were unaware that the Youth Diversion Program even existed. I'm so grateful that they were there when we needed them, to offer my son a second chance.

The Trouble with Tough Love

Maia Szalavitz

As a former drug user and troubled teen, Maia Szalavitz brings a personal perspective to the following viewpoint on residential programs that use so-called tough love. The problem with such programs, she writes, is that most kids who get into trouble do so because of lack of self-esteem, and tough love only adds to kids' self-esteem problems. In addition, she writes, tough love programs can be dangerous, are sometimes run by poorly trained workers, and have not been proven to be effective. Szalavitz is the author of Help at Any Cost: How the Troubled-Teen Industry Cons Parents and Hurts Kids.

It is the ultimate parental nightmare: Your affectionate child is transformed, seemingly overnight, into an out-of-control, drug-addicted, hostile teenager. Many parents blame themselves. "Where did we go wrong?" they ask. The kids, meanwhile, hurtle through their own bewildering adolescent nightmare.

I know. My descent into drug addiction started in high school and now, as an adult, I have a much better understanding of my parents' anguish and of what I was going through. And, after devoting several years to researching treatment programs, I'm also aware of the traps that many parents fall into when they finally seek help for their kids.

Many anguished parents put their faith in strict residential rehab programs. At first glance, these programs, which are commonly based on a philosophy of "tough love," seem to offer a safe respite from the streets—promising reform through confrontational therapy in an isolated environment where kids cannot escape the need to change their behavior. At the same

Maia Szalavitz, "The Trouble With Tough Love," *The Washington Post*, January 29, 2006. Reproduced by permission of the author.

time, during the '90s, it became increasingly common for courts to sentence young delinquents to military-style boot camps as an alternative to incarceration.

But lack of government oversight and regulation makes it impossible for parents to thoroughly investigate services provided by such "behavior modification centers," "wilderness programs" and "emotional growth boarding schools." Moreover, the very notion of making kids who are already suffering go through more suffering is psychologically backwards. And there is little data to support these institutions' claims of success.

Tough Love Is Big Business

Nonetheless, a billion-dollar industry now promotes such tough-love treatment. There are several hundred public and private facilities—both in the United States and outside the country—but serving almost exclusively American citizens. Although no one officially keeps track, my research suggests that some 10,000 to 20,000 teenagers are enrolled each year. A patchwork of lax and ineffective state regulations—no federal rules apply—is all that protects these young people from institutions that are regulated like ordinary boarding schools but that sometimes use more severe methods of restraint and isolation than psychiatric centers. There are no special qualifications required of the people who oversee such facilities. Nor is any diagnosis required before enrollment. If a parent thinks a child needs help and can pay the $3,000- to $5,000-a-month fees, any teenager can be held in a private program, with infrequent contact with the outside world, until he or she turns 18.

Over [a period of] three years, I have interviewed more than 100 adolescents and parents with personal experience in both public and private programs and have read hundreds of media accounts, thousands of Internet postings and stacks of legal documents. I have also spoken with numerous psychiatrists, psychologists, sociologists and juvenile justice experts. Of course there is a range of approaches at different institutions, but most of the people I spoke with agree that the industry is dominated by the idea that harsh rules and even brutal confrontation are necessary to help troubled teenagers. University of California at Berkeley sociologist Elliott Currie, who did an ethnographic study of teen residential addiction treatment for the National Institute on Drug Abuse, told me that he could not think of a program that wasn't influenced by this philosophy.

Unfortunately, tough treatments usually draw public scrutiny only when practitioners go too far, prompting speculation about when "tough is too tough." Dozens of deaths—such as [the 2006] case of 14-year-old Martin Lee Anderson, who died hours after entering a juvenile boot camp that was under contract with Florida's juvenile justice system—and cases of abuse have been documented since tough-love treatment was popularized in the '70s and '80s by programs such as Synanon and Straight, Inc. Parents and teenagers involved with both state-run and private institutions have told me of beatings, sleep deprivation, use of stress positions, emotional abuse and public humiliation, such as making them dress as prostitutes or in drag and addressing them in coarse language. I've heard about the most extreme examples, of course, but the lack of regulation and oversight means that such abuses are always a risk.

The Right Approach?

The more important question—whether tough love is the right approach itself—is almost never broached. Advocates of these programs call the excesses tragic but isolated cases; they offer anecdotes of miraculous transformations to balance the horror stories; and they argue that tough love only *seems* brutal—saying that surgery seems violent, too, without an understanding of its vital purpose.

What advocates don't take from their medical analogy, however, is the principle of "first, do no harm" and the associated requirement of scientific proof of safety and efficacy. Research conducted by the National Institutes of Health and the Department of Justice tells a very different story from the testimonials—one that has been obscured by myths about why addicts take drugs and why troubled teenagers act out.

As a former addict, who began using cocaine and heroin in late adolescence, I have never understood the logic of tough love. I took drugs compulsively because I hated myself, because I felt as if no one—not even my family—would love me if they really knew me. Drugs allowed me to blot out that depressive self-focus and socialize as though I thought I was okay.

How could being "confronted" about my bad behavior help me with that? Why would being humiliated, once I'd given up the only thing that allowed me to feel safe emotionally, make me better? My problem wasn't that I needed to be cut down to size; it was that I felt I didn't measure up.

In fact, fear of cruel treatment kept me from seeking help long after I began to suspect I needed it. My addiction probably could have been shortened if I'd thought I could have found care that didn't conform to what I knew was (and sadly, still is) the dominant confrontational approach.

Fortunately, the short-term residential treatment I underwent was relatively light on confrontation, but I still had to deal with a counselor who tried to humiliate me by disparaging my looks when I expressed insecurity about myself.

Two Problems with Tough Love

The trouble with tough love is twofold. First, the underlying philosophy—that pain produces growth—lends itself to abuse of power. Second, and more important, toughness doesn't begin to address the real problem. Troubled teenagers aren't usually "spoiled brats" who "just need to be taught respect." Like me, they most often go wrong because they hurt, not because they don't want to do the right thing. That became all the more evident to me when I took a look at who goes to these schools.

A surprisingly large number are sent away in the midst of a parental divorce; others are enrolled for depression or other serious mental illnesses. Many have lengthy histories of trauma and abuse. The last thing such kids need is another experience of powerlessness, humiliation and pain.

Sadly, tough love often looks as if it works: For one thing, longitudinal studies find that most kids, even amongst the most troubled, eventually grow out of bad behavior, so the magic of time can be mistaken for the magic of treatment. Second, the experience of being emotionally terrorized can produce compliance that looks like real change, at least initially.

Making Problems Worse

The bigger picture suggests that tough love tends to backfire. My recent interviews confirm the findings of more formal studies. The Justice Department has released reports comparing boot camps with traditional correctional facilities for juvenile offenders, concluding in 2001 that neither facility "is more effective in reducing recidivism." In late 2004, the National Institutes of Health released a "state of the science" consensus statement, concluding that "get tough" treatments "do not work and there is some evidence that they may make the problem worse." Indeed, some young people leave these programs with post-traumatic stress disorder and exacerbations of their original problems.

These strict institutional settings work at cross-purposes with the developmental stages adolescents go through. According to psychiatrists, teenagers need to gain responsibility, begin to test romantic relationships and learn to think critically. But in tough programs, teenagers' choices of activities are overwhelmingly made for them: They are not allowed to date (in many, even eye contact with the opposite sex is punished), and they are punished if they dissent from a program's therapeutic prescriptions. All this despite evidence that a totally controlled environment delays maturation.

Why is tough love still so prevalent? The acceptance of anecdote as evidence is one reason, as are the hurried decisions of desperate parents who can no longer find a way of communicating with their wayward kids. But most significant is the lack of the equivalent of a Food and Drug Administration for behavioral health care—with the result that most people are unaware that these programs have never been proved safe or effective. It's part of what a recent Institute of Medicine report labeled a "quality chasm" between the behavioral treatments known to work and those that are actually available. So parents rely on hearsay—and the word of so-called experts.

Unfortunately, in the world of teen behavioral programs, there are no specific educational or professional requirements. Anyone can claim to be an expert.

My Brother Was Shot

Ayesha

In the following selection, Ayesha, an eighteen-year-old girl in England, writes about her brother being shot. He was eight years older than she was and was often getting into trouble and fighting with their parents. She did not realize how serious the situation was until the night he was shot. Ayesha has dealt with the experience by working with other kids to help them understand the dangers of getting involved with drugs and guns.

My brother Carl was a really cool guy when I was growing up. Because he was eight years older than me, he always really looked after me and stuck up for me.

We weren't in each other's pockets all the time or anything but we were close. I know he used to look out for me.

Mum and dad used to get on at him all the time and at the time I just thought they were getting at him for no reason. I didn't understand what was going on.

It was only much later I found out that Carl was involved in a group of people who were taking drugs on the estate [public housing development] where we lived.

I heard that he'd started hanging around with them when things weren't going well for him at school.

As time went on, the arguments between Carl and my mum and dad got bigger and bigger and eventually Carl stopped sleeping at home as much and sort of moved in with this girl.

They had a baby together but then things didn't work out so Carl was back at ours and the rows [arguments] went on.

Police at the Door

I remember the night we got the knock at the door like it was yesterday. There was a loud banging at the door at about four

Ayesha, "My Brother Was Shot," *Need2Know*, June 30, 2006. Reproduced by permission.

in the morning and at first I thought it was one of Carl's mates [friends] because they used to come at all times of the night.

I looked out of the window and saw it was the police: a man and a woman both wearing uniform. Although Carl seemed to be having problems, he'd never brought the police to my mum's door before.

I waited upstairs while the police talked to mum and dad. When mum started screaming I knew it was bad and so I went downstairs.

Carl had been shot dead at a party by a guy he didn't get on with. It was like a bad dream; I don't really remember much else about that night.

Trying to Understand

As days went by, it just seemed even more weird. Mum wanted to see where Carl had been shot so we went to the place where it happened. People had already started laying flowers in front of the house.

I couldn't speak. I just wanted my brother back.

I felt sorry for his girlfriend and baby; they had needed him to be around for them and he wasn't going to be any more.

Mum just wouldn't stop crying and screaming. I thought the world was about to end.

Since Carl was shot, I've managed to help turn things around. I've talked in our school to other people about the dangers of guns and getting involved in drugs. It has helped me to understand what has happened a bit more.

It's too late for Carl but it's not too late for other people out there. Getting involved in drugs and guns has ruined my family's life and I wouldn't want anybody else to go through what we have.

I don't think I'll ever get over losing Carl but I know that he would have wanted me to do what I'm doing. It can't be ignored.

Others Affected
by Juvenile Crime

A Career in Juvenile Corrections

Francisco "Frank" J. Alarcon, Jr.

Francisco "Frank" J. Alarcon, Jr., wrote the following piece to an-swer those who ask why anyone would want to work in the juve-nile corrections business. He lists the many drawbacks of the job, including low pay, budget cutbacks, and unsatisfied "customers." But, in his mind, the good parts of the job, including the chance to change people's lives in tangible ways, make it worthwhile. Alarcon wrote this while serving as deputy secretary of the Florida Department of Juvenile Justice.

Midway through a recent meeting I was having with a high-level juvenile correctional executive (who shall re-main nameless to protect the guilty) in which we were dis-cussing allegations of staff misconduct, he suddenly paused in mid-sentence and matter-of-factly said, "Why would anyone want to work in this business today?" And with that state-ment, I had the theme for my commentary for this edition of *Corrections Today.*

After all, why *would* anyone want to work in juvenile justice/corrections today? On the surface, anyway, there are certainly many different reasons why country singer Johnny Paycheck's old country standard of "take this job and shove it" might spew out of the mouth of a juvenile corrections proba-tion or parole officer, or a juvenile corrections superintendent, warden or administrator. For purposes of illustration, let's go over a few.

Low Pay and Budget Reductions

Low Pay. There are exceptions, of course, as there are to any of the examples I list here. But for the most part, people who work in juvenile corrections, at all levels, are underpaid and largely underappreciated relative to similar professions. This contributes to an industry with generally high staff turnover, as we see more and more young people move on to higher paying positions in law enforcement, adult corrections or other industries.

Increased Oversight and Scrutiny. Not all of this is bad. In fact, some of us have felt strongly for some time that the juvenile justice system has been severely hampered over the years by its seemingly overindulgent use of the cloak of confidentiality. What I am talking about here is the too common use of juvenile justice and its employees as the scapegoats for everything that is wrong in society. This leads to politicians pontificating to cover their own shortcomings and excessive media "investigations" to sell newspapers and advertising. No wonder the average tenure of a state juvenile correctional administrator is just two years.

Do More with Less. Everyone has had to tighten their belts in this post-9/11 economy and that is fine. And we in juvenile corrections have managed to find intelligent ways to carry out our mandates as well as or better than any other public sector business. However, in state after state, my colleagues inform me that juvenile justice/corrections has taken a disproportionate share of necessary budgetary reductions. Even within all of criminal justice, juvenile corrections usually falls beneath sheriffs, police, the judiciary, state attorneys, public defenders and adult corrections in the pecking order for resources.

Unhappy "Customers." An upset parent calls because his or her child "is not receiving proper treatment" for an ailment that should have been treated before the child was incarcerated. The sheriff is upset because a recent release from detention committed a new crime just two days after his discharge. The state attorney is unhappy because one of your "bleeding heart" probation officers had the audacity to suggest probation for a youth he feels should be locked up. The public defender shares her concern that all your agency ever does is recommend that youths be incarcerated. A judge expresses displeasure over the quality and timeliness of predisposition reports from a probation officer who is carrying 85 active cases. A victim calls and demands a restitution payment. And, by the way, the governor's office is on the phone. They want an answer to a press inquiry and they want it yesterday.

The Good Parts of the Business

Are these exaggerations? No, not at all. Do they tell the whole story? Absolutely not. As someone who has been a proud public servant in his chosen profession during the past 29 years, there are many more reasons I have learned to appreciate why someone would want to work in this business. Read on.

Meaningful Mission. We have the wonderful opportunity to help change people's lives in positive ways. As we have embraced restorative principles and practices, we continue to improve public safety. We assist victims of juvenile crime, help communities strengthen families and neighborhoods, and give young people opportunities to reduce deficits and develop the skills necessary to make it in the real world.

Incredible People. I feel so privileged to have met and to know so many outstanding people from all walks of life who either chose or backed into a career in juvenile justice/ corrections. Committed, conscientious, caring and courageous are just a few of the adjectives that come to mind—and that is just covering the C's in the alphabet. The people in this business are what keeps me going.

Making a Difference

Stimulating Work. The variety of work and challenges is truly amazing. I often tell friends who are less familiar with this business that there is no part of public life that we do not touch or get involved in, whether it is in actual services or by participating in policy-making. As a juvenile correctional administrator, for example, I have been involved in decisions affecting education programs, environmental issues, transportation, construction, health care, private industry, labor, employment, food services—you name it, we either do it or have some influence and involvement.

Interesting Places. Our work takes us to every nook and cranny of our communities—poor and affluent, rural and urban, diverse and homogeneous. We run small six-bed group homes and large 1,000-bed facilities. We see courtrooms and boardrooms and visit the YMCA and jail. Some of us even take or get the opportunity to conduct site visits in other states and countries.

Fascinating Future. We know so much more today about "what works" than we knew 30, 20 and even 10 years ago. Evidence- and research-based approaches to reducing juvenile crime and improving recidivism rates are gaining in acceptance and implementation. We are getting better at targeting our prevention resources for high-risk children before they have serious involvement in the system. We are improving our screening and assessment tools to better understand both the strengths and weaknesses of the families and young people we see. We are doing a better job of training our work force to meet the challenges of juvenile crime in the new millennium.

A Student Threatened My School on the Internet

Allison Ko

In the following selection, sixteen-year-old Allison Ko describes what it was like to be at her school in the days after a student posted threats against her school on the Internet. The threat named several students who would be targeted and warned them not to come to school. She describes the initial confusion as students were not told exactly why there were police at the school and how student reactions changed throughout the day. She also talks to one of the threatened students who talks about her fear and the poor way the police handled the situation. Ko is a student at Wilson High School in Hacienda Heights, California, near Los Angeles.

On Wednesday, April 16, [2008] a threat against my school was posted on Wikipedia. Targeting several students as well as the school's badminton team, the threat said that there was going to be a shooting at my school on Friday, April 18. Students who were named on the hit list were told not to come to school. The rest of us did not know about the threat until the next morning. When I got to school, I was confused and had no idea what was going on. As I found out about the threat, I was more shocked than scared. I usually heard about stuff like this in the news, but I never imagined that it would happen to me at my school.

Thursday started out like a normal school day—I was in a rush, hoping not to be late for the second time in a week. At the gate where my dad always drops me off, there was a security guard blocking our way. My dad drove me to the main entrance, where I saw a long line of students.

Allison Ko, "It Was Frightening When a Student Made an Internet Threat Against My School," *L.A. Youth*, March-April 18, 2008. Reproduced by permission.

There were police cars everywhere and all the gate entrances to the school were blocked, so that no cars could come in. Policemen were searching our bags. My classmates were getting scanned with a metal detector. What the heck was going on?

After about 40 minutes, it was finally my turn. The police told me to open my book bag and stand in line for a security guard to search me with a metal detector. My friend asked a police officer what the reason was behind all this. He explained that it was confidential.

Not Told What Was Happening

In my zero period class, our teacher explained that something had happened the previous night. He told us that he didn't know much yet, but assured us that we were safe. Walking to our first period class, my friends and I looked out the school gate and saw a huge line of students, even longer than when I first got to school.

In my first period only about seven students out of nearly 35 were in the classroom. The teacher turned on a movie for us to watch. People were coming in one by one; yet there were still some empty seats. I talked to one of the editors of the school newspaper staff, Jenny, about whether we should be taking pictures of the line of students and the bag searches. We decided to go. Administrators and faculty members were all around the school, telling students to go to their first period classes.

"Where are you girls going?" one counselor asked us. "You girls need to be at your first period class."

Jenny took me to her friend's first period, a senior math class. The teacher and the students were talking about the threat. They said that Homeland Security and the FBI were involved. At that moment, I knew I should have stayed in my first period classroom. I nearly ran back to my first period class because I didn't want the counselor to catch me again. I felt that something serious was happening if all the adults were making sure we were in class.

In second period, my teacher explained to us that last night, a threat against specific students was posted on an Internet site. These students were told to stay home. My classmate and I looked at each other, eyes wide. Hacienda Heights is a peaceful neighborhood where nothing ever goes wrong. Stuff like this wasn't supposed to happen here.

Some students weren't at school—students who were in my classes, students who were my friends. There were rumors that these absent students were probably on the hit list. Did something happen to them? Were they on the list? Why weren't they here?

During the day a letter from the principal was read to us. It explained the situation and assured that we would be safe. Later, we were notified that school would be closed Friday and after-school activities would be postponed.

After school, my friends and I learned more. There were two threats posted. The first one said there would be a shooting at our school. It was removed, and a second threat was posted. I later searched for the threat but I couldn't find the post because it had already been taken down. Instead, I found an image of it on the *Whittier Daily News'* website. It read:

"You removed my last edit. I gave you a fair warning. Now the people listed in my previous edit will be victims in the Glen A. Wilson Shooting to occur this Friday. Your lack of attention to the seriousness of my warning will now be the reason as to why you will receive all fault of this event. Be prepared to have 33 families mourn the loss of their children and place a lawsuit upon your shoulders."

I felt a chill running down my spine. It sounded like something awful could have happened. Yet, at the same time, I had doubts. Was the person who posted the threats really serious? Could he have actually done something like this? My friends and I were curious why someone would post something like this in the first place. Some of us didn't want to know who had threatened these students. The person could have been a classmate, a lab partner or someone we encountered daily.

The next day, I got a call from my friend with good news. She told me that the guy who threatened the school had been arrested, but no one knew who it was. Because he was a minor, his name was not released. I didn't care who it was—I was just glad that it was over.

On Monday at school one of my friends told me that she had been named on the hit list. She told me how scared she was. She said that Thursday morning before school there was a voicemail from the police.

"My heart was pumping," she said. "The voicemail was very specific. It said, 'Do not take your daughter to school today. This is for her safety.'"

The police told her to stay home that day and the next day. Detectives came to her house to ask her a few questions, then she was told to come to the police station to answer more questions. "That was the worst part of the whole experience," she said.

She said one cop treated her very harshly. The cop said to her, "Who would do this to you? I can see it in your eyes. I can see you're nervous. I know you know!"

The cop even asked her if she was the one who posted the threats.

"I was hysterical," she said, "I couldn't believe that she even asked me that."

The next day, she went to the Buddhist temple.

"That's how scared I was," she said, "I'm not a religious person, and for me to go the temple and pray—that's a crazy thing for me."

Around 3 P.M. she got a call from her friend, who told her there had been an arrest.

"I was so mad that the police didn't call. The arrest had been made at 11:30 A.M., and I had to find out from a friend about three hours later," she said. "I was upset that I had worried for an extra three hours."

It was frightening, but at the same time, many of us wondered how seriously we should take this threat. A lot of it seemed make-believe because stuff like this usually happened in the movies. The news was all over the media—we were on TV, in the newspapers and on the Internet. Our school's name appeared on national headlines. This made everything seem more real and serious. Before, shootings like those at Virginia Tech and Columbine High School seemed unreal, but now I have a different perspective.

I think the school did the best they could to keep us safe. Everyone eventually found out what was going on and so I can't say that we weren't informed. Although I was scared, I don't think I ever felt as if I was in danger. Many students are saying that the person behind the threat did not mean what he posted online. However, it's too risky to ignore something like that. As scary as it sounds, I think something like this could have happened at any school. I'm not trying to scare anyone. All I'm saying is that we need to be safe and take threats seriously.

Teaching a Writing Class at a Juvenile Detention Center

Kim Antieau

In the following selection, writer Kim Antieau describes her visit to a juvenile detention center to talk about writing. She is nervous but notices that the teens seem alert and interested in hearing about the life of a writer. Few have read her books, so Antieau gives an impromptu lesson by having the class write a one hundred word story together. The students enthusiastically jump in with suggestions and come up with a group story. "I don't know if they got anything from the visit," writes Antieau, "but I was glad to be with them, glad to hear their voices." Antieau's sixth novel, Ruby's Imagine, *was published in 2008.*

I went to juvenile detention today to talk about writing. I won't tell you the city or anyone's name or even describe anyone I met very carefully so that I don't reveal anything that might be considered private.

Lucy (not her real name; she invited me to speak to the students in detention) drove us to juvenile detention, which was right downtown (not my town). It was a kind of nondescript government building. Not very noticeable. Lucy pressed a buzzer (although I didn't hear it buzz) at the door. I heard a mumble through the speaker—like at a fast food drive-up— and Lucy said her name. Then she pushed the door open. We went down a short hallway past a darkened room. Inside, two people in uniform sat at a console, a man and a woman. Lucy said something to me or them, and we kept walking. Got buzzed in through another door. And another. And another. Four doors all together, I think.

Then we walked down a long sloping hallway. I wanted to be very observant, take it all in, but I was listening to Lucy tell

Kim Antieau, "Juvie," *The Furious Spinner*, October 25, 2005. Reproduced by permission of the author.

me about the place and the children, and I was fascinated. The juveniles within had committed various crimes: theft, assault, drugs, molestation, and murder. She told me one or two boys might be in the classroom today. Sometimes it was overflow, sometimes the boys who had molested other boys were put in with the girls for their own protection. Apparently since they molested other boys, they weren't considered a threat to the girls.

Inside the "Pod"

We walk into the "pod," where the girls lived. It reminded me of the cell block area in the cable series *Oz*, except smaller. Cells around an open area. (On one door, someone had taped that series of photos of a meth addict you see at nearly every police station: first she was beautiful, then ugly, then uglier, then pitted and old and even uglier. It's the best anti-drug ad I've ever seen, although I don't know if it does any good. Meth is a problem everywhere in the PNW [Pacific Northwest].) An open staircase led up to the second floor of cells. Three picnic tables (of a sort) in the middle of the room on the bottom floor, each with a checker/chess board as part of it on one end.

At the end of the pod, we went through a door into a classroom that looked like any other classroom, only the students were dressed in institutional garb: the girls in dark blue, the boys in gold. Four boys sat in the desks along the farthest wall, across from the door. Girls sat in the other three rows of chairs. The teacher and Lucy talked a bit. I stood at the door looking around, a little nervous. Fourteen students. One Black, one Asian, the rest appeared to be Anglo. Four boys; ten girls. Ages: between 10 and 17? Most of them were probably 15 and 16. One girl was so small and looked so young it almost hurt to look at her, to imagine why she was here.

Lucy introduced me, and I began with, "I'm not as old as I look. I got gray hair when I was a teenager." They seemed amused by this.

I asked how many of them had read *Mercy, Unbound*. One girl raised her hand and said she was in the process of reading it. The other girls who had read it were gone for various reasons. So I started talking about writing and why I wrote instead of having a discussion about *Mercy*, which I had planned. They seemed alert, listening, responsive. One or two looked very tired. I asked if anyone had questions, but no one asked anything except Lucy and the teacher. They wanted to know how much I made on one book and how I actually got a book published. I told them how much I was paid, and I said that actually getting a book published was generally a long hideous process. I should have been more specific, but talking about that part of writing is really boring to me, so I steered the conversation toward other topics. I read a bit of *Mercy* out loud. (I picked the wrong section, and it didn't work that well). Then one of the students asked me how to get started writing. She liked to write but she had trouble getting started.

Writing Together

"My husband writes an entire story in one hundred words, each day," I said. "That's a good way to start. Look at other books and see how they start. I started *Mercy* with 'Call me Mercy.' I got that from Herman Melville's book *Moby Dick*. It starts out 'Call me Ishmael.' *David Copperfield* begins with 'I was born.' My book *The Jigsaw Woman* begins with 'I was born.' But I put a twist on it. 'I was born. In a crossfire of hurricanes. Or something.' Do you know what part of that is from?" They shook their heads. "Heard of the Rolling Stones?" I began singing, "I was born in a cross fire of hurricanes." They laughed. "In fact, let's do that now. We'll write a hundred word story. Let's start with 'I was born.' What's next?"

This got the students going. I encouraged them to call out lines.

Here are snippets of how it went. At one point I read, "I was born in Brooklyn, New York, the third child of twenty-four children. My mother was very tired. She had wrinkles and seizures. On the third day after her twenty-fourth child was born, my mother died. I took care of my 23 siblings with my drunken father."

"Only twenty-one siblings," one boy said.

"Why?" I asked.

Several of them said, "Because she was the third child."

I looked at them blankly (for a split second, this was all happening quickly).

One said, "Why would she take care of her two older brothers and sisters?"

"Good point," I said. I was impressed. They were paying better attention than I was.

I walked along the rows as I wrote out what they said. It was exhilarating to have them talking, participating. I didn't edit what they said. I wrote it and read it.

"Does she have *a* drug problem or drug problems?" I asked when someone shouted out the sentence.

"Multiple drug problems!" several said.

The Class Story

I read it out loud again—and again, each time we added a sentence, until we got to here:

I was born in Brooklyn, New York, the third child of twenty-four children. My mother was very tired. She had wrinkles and seizures. On the third day after her twenty-fourth child was born, my mother died. I took care of my twenty-one siblings with my drunken father. We got child support, and I had drug problems. CPS [child protection services] came and took away my brothers and sisters. I got away. I lived on the streets and sold dope.

"So now we need to think about this in storytelling terms," I said. "You can do whatever you like as a storyteller, but as of right now, are you rooting for this character?"

"No!" I heard.

"So do you want to do anything about that?"

"We can make it all turn out later," one girl said.

"No, there's no happily ever after in life," another said.

"So how do we end this?" I asked.

"She was killed in a drive-by shooting," a boy said.

"She got a boyfriend and they lived happily together." A girl.

"A boyfriend doesn't solve anything." A girl. "She gets a girlfriend."

"She becomes a dope lord." Girl.

"She electrocutes the boyfriend and goes to prison." A girl.

"She has twenty-one children and was very tired." A boy.

"Actually, as a storytelling device," I said. "That is very clever. It brings it all around again."

"How could she have twenty-one children if she was with a girl?" A girl. Same girl.

"They could have a surrogate or something." Another girl.

"She escaped to Canada and lived happily ever after."

To Be Continued?

"I tell you what," I said. "I want you each to come up with your own ending. If your teacher will do it with you later, I want to see what you come up with."

"Can we change what we already have?" A girl.

"Absolutely," I said. I thought, "That's what it's all about, sugar."

I gave them copies of *Coyote Cowgirl*. And then we left. I don't know if they got anything from the visit, but I was glad to be with them, glad to hear their voices.

Organizations to Contact

The editors have compiled the following list of organizations concerned with the issues debated in this book. The descriptions are derived from materials provided by the organizations. All have publications or information available for interested readers. The list was compiled on the date of publication of the present volume; the information provided here may change. Be aware that many organizations take several weeks or longer to respond to inquiries, so allow as much time as possible.

American Youth Work Center (AYWC)
1200 17th St. NW, 4th Floor, Washington, DC   20036
(202) 785-0764 • fax: (678) 387-0101
e-mail: info@youthtoday.org
Web site: http://www.aywc.org

The American Youth Work Center assists the staff and management of youth service organizations in the U.S. and abroad with the goal of improving services to children and youth. It advocates for increased funding for at-risk youth, offers training programs and publishes youth work publications. AYWC publishes the magazine, *Youth Today: The Newspaper on Youth Work.*

Boys Hope Girls Hope
12120 Bridgeton Square Dr., Bridgeton, MO   63044-2607
(314) 298-1250 • fax: (314) 298-1251
e-mail: hope@bhgh.org
Web site: www.boyshopegirlshope.org

Boys Hope Girls Hope provides aid to families and youth. It offers counseling, education, and long term housing to youth who wish to succeed but lack a supportive home life. The organization publishes the newsletter, *Voice of HOPE*, which highlights the lives of successful alumni.

Center on Juvenile and Criminal Justice (CJCJ)
440 9th St., San Francisco, CA   94103
(415) 621-5661 • fax: (415) 621-5466
e-mail: dmacallair@cjcj.org
Web site: www.cjcj.org

The Center on Juvenile and Criminal Justice was established to promote balanced and humane criminal justice policies that reduce incarceration and promote long-term public safety. CJCJ's mission is pursued through the development of model programs, technical assistance, research/policy analysis, and public education. The organization offers many publications including "Crime Rates and Youth Incarceration in Texas and California Compared: Public Safety or Public Waste?"

Children Now
1212 Broadway, 5th Floor, Oakland, CA   94612
(510) 763-2444 • fax: (510) 763-1974
e-mail: info@childrennow.org
Web site: www.childrennow.org

Children Now is a research and advocacy group that works on ensuring that children are the top public policy priority. The group focuses on health care, education, child care and positive media for children. Children Now publishes the *California County Data Book*.

Coalition for Juvenile Justice (CJJ)
1710 Rhode Island Ave. NW, 10th Floor
Washington, DC   20036
(202) 467-0864 • fax: (202) 887-0738
e-mail: info@juvjustice.org
Web site: www.juvjustice.org

The Coalition for Juvenile Justice represents government appointed juvenile justice advisory groups from the United States. The organization's goals include: instituting reforms in the juvenile justice system, educating the pubic on juvenile justice issues and aiding states in meeting the requirements of the Juvenile Justice and Delinquency Prevention Act. CJJ publishes the newsletter, *AssemblyLine.*

Fresh Lifelines for Youth (FLY)
120 W Mission St., San Jose, CA   95110
(408) 263-2630
e-mail: christa@flyprogram.org
Web site: www.flyprogram.org

Fresh Lifelines for Youth encourages teens in trouble to make healthy decisions by offering at-risk and disadvantaged youth education about the law, mentoring and leadership training programs. The group advocates education, attention and mentoring as the best ways to keep kids out of prison.

Office of Juvenile Justice and Delinquency Prevention (OJJDP)
810 Seventh Street, NW, Washington, DC   20531
(202) 307-5911 • fax: (202) 307-2093
e-mail: Askjj@ncjrs.org
Web site: ojjdp.ncjrs.org

The Office of Juvenile Justice and Delinquency Prevention provides national leadership, coordination, and resources to prevent and respond to juvenile delinquency and victimization. OJJDP supports states and communities in their efforts to develop and implement prevention and intervention programs and to improve the juvenile justice system so that it protects public safety, holds offenders accountable, and provides treatment and rehabilitative services tailored to the needs of juveniles and their families. The organization publishes the journal *Juvenile Justice.*

National Commission on Correctional Health Care (NCCHC)
1145 W Diversey Pkwy., Chicago, IL   60614
(773) 880-1460 • fax: (773) 880-2424

e-mail: info@ncchc.org
Web site: www.ncchc.org

The mission of the National Commission on Correctional Health Care is to improve the quality of health care in jails, prisons and juvenile confinement facilities. It offers accreditation, training and seminars for correctional care health facilities and issue Standards for Health Services, which offers recommendations for improving medical and mental health care in correctional institutions. CCHP publishes the journal *CorrectCare*.

The Pendulum Foundation
5082 E. Hampden Ave, #192, Denver, CO   80222
(720) 314-1402
e-mail: pendulumfoundation.com
Web site: www.pendulumfoundation.com

The Pendulum Foundation educates the public on child welfare and juvenile justice issues. It advocates on behalf of children, especially those in trouble with the law. The Web site offers testimonials, information and resources on youth and issues of justice.

Voices for America's Children
1000 Vermont Ave. NW, Ste. 700, Washington, DC   20005
(202) 289-0777 • fax (202) 289-0776
e-mail: voices@voices.org
Web site: www.voicesforamericaschildren.org

Voices for America's Children is a network of child advocacy groups. It seeks to maximize the effectiveness of such groups in their key policy goals of equity, health, school readiness, school success, safety and economic stability. The Web site offers a database of publications on topics such as juvenile justice, child poverty and community mobilization.

Youth Law Center (YLC)
Children's Legal Protection Center, San Francisco, CA 94104
(415) 543-3379 • fax: (415) 956-9022
e-mail: info@youthlawcenter.com
Web site: www.ylc.org

The Youth Law Center is a public interest law firm that works
to protect children in the nation's foster care and juvenile justice systems from abuse and neglect, and to ensure that they
receive the necessary support and services to become healthy
and productive adults. The firm provides litigation, education
and advocacy on juvenile justice law. YLC's Web site offers fact
sheets on a variety of issues concerning child welfare and juvenile justice.

For Further Research

Books

Gordon Cruse, *Juvie: Inside Canada's Youth Jails*. Vancouver, BC: Granville Island, 2007.

R. Barri Flowers, *Kids Who Commit Adult Crimes: Serious Criminality by Juvenile Offenders*. New York: Routledge, 2002.

Debbie J. Goodman and Ron Grimming, *Juvenile Justice: A Collection of True-Crime Cases*. Upper Saddle River, NJ: Prentice Hall, 2007.

Thomas A. Jacobs, *Teens Take It to Court: Young People Who Challenged the Law—and Changed Your Life*. Minneapolis: Free Spirit, 2006.

Luis J. Rodriguez, *La Vida Loca: Gang Days in L.A.* New York: Touchstone, 2005

Sanyika Sakur, *Monster: The Autobiography of an L.A. Gang Member*. Jackson, TN: Grove, 2004.

Laurie Schaffner, *Girls in Trouble with the Law*. Piscataway, NJ: Rutgers University Press, 2006.

Seventeen Magazine, Seventeen Real Girls, Real-Life Stories: True Crime. New York: Hearst, 2007.

Colton Simpson and Ann Pearlman, *Inside the Crips: Life Inside L.A.'s Most Notorious Gang*. New York: St. Martin's, 2005.

Youth Communication, *In Too Deep: Teens Write About Gangs*. New York: Youth Communication, 2005.

Periodicals

Shannon Agofsky, "Profile," *Death Row Speaks*, January 9, 2007. www.deathrowspeaks.info/inmates/shannonagof sky.html.

Anonymous, "From Victim—to Perpetrator—to Victim," Operation Awareness, 2008. www.operationawareness .com.about_1_child.html.

Cheryl Armstrong, "Kids in Colorado," Pendulum Foundation, January 2008. www.pendulumfoundation.com/ coloradokids.html.

Maggie Burks, "Eating Their Own Vomit," *Jackson (MS) Free Press*, November 7, 2007. www.jacksonfreepress .com/index.php/site/comments/eating_their_own_vomit/.

L.Z. Granderson, "No Substitute for Being There," *ESPN Page 2*, March 29, 2007. http://sports.espn.go.com/espn/ page2/story?page=granderson/070329.

Thomas Grisso, "Progress and Perils in the Juvenile Justice and Mental Health Movement," *Journal of the American Academy of Psychiatry and the Law*, June 1, 2007.

G. Grissom, "Juvenile Crime: A Problem of the Delinquent Child or the 'Delinquent' Parent?" *Socyberty*, August 4, 2008. www.socyberty.com/Law/Juvenile-Crime-A-Problem-of-the-Delinquent-Child-or-the-Delinquent-Parent.195199.

Christopher Hartney, "Native American Youth and the Juvenile Justice System," *Focus*, March 2008. www.nccd-crc.org/nccd/pubs/2008_Focus_NativeAmerican.pdf.

Peter Landesman,"L.A. Gangs: Nine Miles and Spreading," *L.A. Weekly*, December 13, 2007. www.laweekly.com/ 2007-12-13/news/l-a-gangs-nine-miles-and-spreading/1.

Sylvia Moreno, "In Texas, Scandals Rock Juvenile Justice System," *Washington Post*, April 5, 2007. www.washingtonpost.com/wp-dyn/content/article/2007/04/04/AR2007040402400.html.

New York Times, "When 'Tough Love' Is Too Tough," October 16, 2007. www.nytimes.com/2007/10/16/opinion/16tue3.html.

Sharon Noguchi, "School Administrators Police Clothing on Campuses: Schools Ban Clothing Linked to Gangs," *San Jose (CA) Mercury News*, September 2, 2008. www.mercurynews.com/education/ci_10365210?nclick_check=1.

Colin Poitras, "Teen Crimes, Adult Prisons," *Hartford (CT) Courant*, February 21, 2006. www.courant.com/news/local/hc-juvage0221.artfeb21,0,2929623.story?coll=hc-headlines-local.

Matthew Quirk, "How to Grow a Gang," *Atlantic Monthly*, May 2008. www.theatlantic.com/doc/200805/world-in-numbers.

Wendy Thomas Russell, "Many Answers, No Easy Fixes," *Long Beach (CA) Press-Telegram*, May 25, 2008. www.presstelegram.com/news/ci_9362427.

Maia Szalavitz, "What Works for Troubled Teens?" *Mother Jones*, August 2007. www.motherjones.com/news/feature/2007/09/non_shocking_therapy.html.

Elizabeth Ulrich, "Handle with Care: The State Continues to License a Midstate Youth Treatment Facility Where Two Have Died and Many Others Have Been Abused," *Nashville Scene*, November 8, 2007. www.nashvillescene.com/2007-11-08/news/handle-with-care/.

Andre Vaughn, "Andre's Story," *Youth Portraits*, January 2002. http://youthportraits.org/andre.php3

Adam Young, "After-School Programs Target Juvenile Crime," Texas Technical University *Daily Toreador*, November 14, 2007. http://media.www.dailytoreador.com/media/storage/paper870/news/2007/11/14/News/After School.Programs.Target.Juvenile.Crime-3098843.shtml

Index

M.N., 40–41
R.A., 44–45
Ricky, 31
Steffi, 37–38
Whyte, Yovani, 27–33
Center on Juvenile and Criminal
 Justice (CJCJ), 75
Child protection services, 71
Child support, 72
Children Now, 75
Church, 41
CJCJ (Center on Juvenile and
 Criminal Justice), 75
Coalition for Juvenile Justice
 (CJJ), 75–76
Cocaine, 53
Columbine High School shoot-
 ings, 68
Community programs, 11, 47, 48,
 49
Community service, 11, 48
Compton (CA), 41
Confrontation, 53
Cops. *See* Police
Corporan, Ariel (case study),
 14–21
Corrections Today (publication), 60
Counselors, 53
Courts, 10, 48, 49
Coyote Cowgirl (Antieau), 73
Crack dealing, 17, 18
Crimes
 assault, 16, 22
 burglaries, 36
 crack dealing, 17, 18
 drug dealing/hustling, 16–19
 identity theft, 37
 kidnapping, 36
 misdemeanors, 28
 robbery, 27, 28, 30, 36–38

school shootings, 68
shoplifting, 34, 46–47
Crown Heights, Brooklyn (NY),
 27
Currie, Elliott, 52
CYA (California Youth Authority),
 41–44

D

Daniella (case study), 30, 32
David Copperfield (Dickens), 71
Day camps, 40–45
D.C. (case study), 42–43
Deaths, 57
Department of Justice, 10, 53
Depression, 54
Divorce, 54
Dope, 17
Driving without consent, 44
Drugs
 boredom and, 36, 38
 cocaine, 53
 dealing/hustling, 16–19
 guns and, 57
 heroin, 36–37
 homelessness and, 23–24
 marijuana, 35
 methamphetamines, 36, 70
 treatment programs for, 25,
  52
D.U. (case study), 43–44

E

Eduardo (case study), 28, 29, 30,
 32
"Emotional growth boarding
 schools," 51
Employment, 36, 37, 43, 44, 45